D1014989

BLACK IMAGINATION

McSWEENEY'S
SAN FRANCISCO

McSweeney's and colophon are registered trademarks of McSweeney's, an independent publisher based in San Francisco.

Cover art: Vanessa German, "I Will Not Suffer For You," 2017. Mixed-media assemblage, 70 × 44 × 6 inches. Courtesy of the artist and Pavel Zoubok Fine Art, NY. Photo: Concept Art Gallery, Pittsburgh, PA

Printed in Canada.

ISBN: 978-1-944211-84-4

10 9 8 7 6 5 4 3 2 1

www.mcsweeneys.net

BLACK IMAGINATION

CURATED BY

NATASHA MARIN

McSWEENEY'S
SAN FRANCISCO

INTERLUDE: RITUALS

CODA: RITUALS

ORIGINS

FOREWORD

Black Imagination is a book that listens while it tells and questions while it answers, and then when the silt settles, it muddies the waters again. Each voice (sharing this space equally) offers unique insight into what it means to imagine and to heal, as well as what "origins" themselves mean. In this way, it's cyclical: not a perfect cycle, but a cycle like the turbulence of pouring cream into coffee. Blackness is expanded, layered, multiple, and lush like we already know it is, but which isn't always recognized and valued by whiteness.

We know how we exist in the white imagination. But this book isn't about that—about constantly correcting ourselves, tiptoeing around, and placating whiteness. It is about saying and doing what we need/want to imagine and heal. Black Imagination is a reclamation of our bodies, space, intelligence, care, and joy. Black Imagination is a reclamation of our whole damn selves. It's connection and kinship. A celebration of *us*.

But don't think for one minute that Black Imagination is easy. As you will read here, it is hard-earned and sometimes dangerous, but it's necessary, and radical, to claim and work towards. Listening to my people in this book gave me so much life, and I'm pretty sure, dear reader, you're in for the same.   —*Steven Dunn*

INTRODUCTION

I experienced Black Imagination last night and found it to be very relaxing. But I think that's because I'm black, and so the black voices and music in the dark maze of the exhibit did not challenge my auditory and tactile senses, but soothed them. This may not be the case for a white person, because a large part of the ideology that, from day one, structured my senses (how I see, feel, and hear things) had the goal of coding a person who viewed me as dangerous, inferior, from a shithole, and even non-human.

So, my choice was either to reject this ideology or to hate myself. This was not a hard choice to make. But if the ideology glorified the color of your skin, and negated those who did not look like you, rejecting it is no simple or easy matter. This is why the experience of Black Imagination might actually be jarring or disorienting if you are white.

—Charles Mudede on "Black Imagination: The States of Matter," *The Stranger*, Jan 12, 2018

I am healthy, whole, and black at the same time.

In 2016, I launched a project called *Reparations* that endeavored to create a space for people who might not otherwise connect to cross networks and racial boundaries in order to share resources. The project encouraged people of color to make requests for what might bring about some present-day repair/healing for race-based trauma and financial inequality, while "white-identified" individuals were asked to leverage their privilege by responding to these requests and by making offerings to do something real and meaningful for members of the wider community (who suffer directly from the increasingly polarized racial climate). My genuine naiveté kept me from realizing that the word "reparations" all by itself triggers racists. The project was introduced to the wider public via Facebook and within 72 hours had reached over 100,000 people worldwide—within six months, a quarter of a million people were engaged. I could not have anticipated this kind of response. My inbox and my life was flooded with the kind of intensity that can only be rendered in metaphor. But that wouldn't do justice to the specificity and the magnitude of need, generosity, and, most surprisingly, the hate I found myself on the receiving end of. Never in my life had any of my idea-actualizations commanded so much ire—death threats, doxxing, trolling of every kind. I was called *nigger* about a hundred times before breakfast each day. Even three years later, I still receive hate-filled messages regularly. This took its toll. My children missed me. I had no time.

In 2018, in order to make reparations to myself for my *Reparations* project, I read only the words of black women and savored the sticky stain left by minds like N.K. Jemisin, Nnedi Okorafor, and Tomi Adeyemi. For me, the joyful escape into this Black Imagination was both profound and liberating. I suppose, for someone else, it might be like suddenly becoming vegan, but instead of cutting out meat, dairy, and animal products from my diet and feeling amazing, I was cutting out White Supremacist ideation as filtered through what I was reading specifically, but also with an eye to all forms of popular media and visual exchange.

Between this chasm and The Now is a wide gulf of joy and I am presently lying in the sunshine of a beach named Unbothered. I swam through a million emails to get here—my arms aching and muscles knotted, even in my sleep. But I got here. And here's how I did it:

I joined forces with other black women (Amber Flame, Rachael Ferguson, and Imani Sims) who already have too much to do. We planned an exhibition that would de-center Whiteness and provide space for healing and validation. We agreed to collect sound from black folks of all kinds, and craving nuance over stereotype, we sought out black children, black youth, LGBTQ+ black folks, unsheltered black folks, incarcerated black folks, neurodivergent black folks, as well as differently-abled black folks. Using field recorders, we spent months collecting responses to three prompts:

What is your origin story?

How do you heal yourself?

Describe/Imagine a world where you are loved, safe, and valued.

After a few months, there was grant funding available to allow us to create an exhibition/experience at the CORE Gallery in

Seattle. Instead of the visual arts exhibition many were expecting, upon arrival, blindfolded guests entered a pitch-black space, and docent, Ayanna Hobson—a nationally recorded vocalist—led them through a sonic web of the collected voices combined with her own exquisitely beautiful one.

These testimonies here are healing me. They are the sun and I am the sand and the sparkle is black joy. I am so honored to have been a witness.

close your eyes—
make the white
gaze disappear.

This book is dedicated to my children—Roman and Sagan—my only real legacy ... and to the beauty, strength, and enduring resilience of Black People everywhere.

Special Thanks to my family for generously protecting me and bringing me this far with primordial love—my mother, Patricia Marin; my father, David Marin; my older (and wiser) sister, Nikola Marin—without you all, who would I even be?

DEAREST BLACK READER, HERE IS MY LOIN-FRUIT. MY FIRSTBORN ... LITERALLY.

AGE 7

My name is Empire Red.

My Mother's name is Luminous Red.

My Father's name is Ambidextrous Red—to his face, I call him
Mammoth Red and behind his back, I call him Juvenile Red.

I come from people known for being in charge, who don't like to
be told what to do.

Remember me.

AGE 9

My name is Sorry Not Sorry Red.

My mother's name is Truth Be Told Red.

My father's name is Ambidextrous Red.

My brother's name is Monkeytown Red.
 I come from a people known for making a moment worth
    something
& being able to tell you off like no one's business.
Remember me.

AGE 12

My name is Continental, Gives You Life Although You Don't
    Notice Red.
My Mother's name is I've Killed Everyone Who's Tried To Chop
    Me Down Red.
My Father's name is The Battle To Remain Ambidextrous Red.
My Brother's name is In Everyone's Mouth Even Though They
    Don't Deserve The Right To Call Upon His Genius Yet Red.
Apparently, I come from people known for long names, the word
    "intricate," and long histories.
Remember me.

AGE 14

My name is Give Me What I Deserve Red.
My Mother's name is Decolonize Moisturize Get What's Yours
    Red.
My Father's name is Never Not Gonna Be Ambidextrous Red.
My Brother's name is More Than You Know Red to you, but to
    me, he is Thing Two Red.

I come from people known for pretty words and the highest
  podiums.
Remember Me.

Roman O'Brien
Seattle, WA, USA

7 STEPS FOR THE
WHITE-IDENTIFIED READER

STEP 1: RELAX.

You have claimed all the things already, except silence. Except for all the seats in the world. Feel free to have them—it is, of course, your birthright.

STEP 2: BREATHE.

STEP 3: IMAGINE.

Your brain is a puckered little sphincter resting on your shoulders and you now have less than a pinch of pages to cram something new and precious into it before the cops arrive. In this fantasy, you are Black. So you know the cops shoot first and ask questions never, so hurry up and relax your mental sphincter.

But you're White, right?
So no matter what, you'll be ok.

STEP 4: AVOID.

Do not ask yourself how you got this way, ask your grandparents.
This may require a ritual of some kind.

STEP 5: CONSIDER.

If you hold a stone in your cheek for 1,000 years, will there still be
a cheek and a separate stone?

STEP 6: REALIZE.

Everything calling itself "White" is a description of lack.

STEP 7: REASSURE YOURSELF.[1]

Your insistence on your own "Whiteness" means that you are
indeed accustomed to believing a factless and fictional narrative
that positions you as superior and central to all validated narratives.

---

1 That's my nice way of saying: I might have to leave you as ignorant
as I found you, James, John, Michael, Robert, William, David, Richard,
Mary, Patty, Jennifer, Linda, Liz, Barb, Susan, Jessica, Sarah,* et al.

*Popular [white] birth names 1918–2017
https://www.ssa.gov/oact/babynames/decades/century.html

IMAGINE

Malcolm: "Do you have candy or regrets?"

Amber: "I have neither candy, nor regrets."

SERENITY WISE
AUCKLAND, NEW ZEALAND

When I imagine a place where I feel safe and loved it's completely unrealistic—so not really that relatable to this world. And the closest thing is when I'm at home alone in my kind of quiet space. Nobody knows that I'm taking the whole day to just sit in my pajamas and be by myself. It's hard for me to imagine a realistic world as a human where I feel safe and loved, you know, completely. It's always like a partial thing when you walk around the human world. But in my imagination I'm a water molecule and a river and an ocean. I'm heavy. That feels like a safe space and a loving space because it's natural and I think that it's natural to be in a space where you're safe and loved. It feels like that should be a natural experience.

REAGAN JACKSON
SEATTLE, WA, USA

When I wake up there is someone there who loves me. When I leave my home the people living on my street know my name, know my parents' names, name and claim me as their own, drop by with soup when I am sick and small gifts during holidays. And I do the same for them. We break bread together. We laugh and dance and work and build together. Wherever I go I am known and I know others. We greet each other with smiles and hugs. Our expressions are always genuine. We don't hide resentments between clenched teeth or anger in clenched fists. We say the words that need saying. We speak and listen and forgive and understand. We are peaceful in our hearts and actions and our peace is never built on the sacrifice of another's peace. Our community is not built on the suffering of others. We live in balance, never taking more than we need, never needing so much we can't sustain ourselves. And each of us are honored and valued and respected as equal members of a collective irrespective of age, ability, ethnicity, gender, or any other political descriptor. We bring all of who we are.

EBO BARTON
SEATTLE, WA, USA

In a world where I feel safe, valued, and loved

There would be skyscrapers

Filled with chairs where

Cisgender

Able-Bodied

Affluent

Straight

White

Men

(and Women)

Could take several seats.

For months at a time.

We'd call them greenhouses.

To ensure their growth (and sweat) from sitting down.

Black and Indigenous Women (Trans Women are Women)
Would burn down what they wished.
After taking a long vacation from not having (certain) people
    around.
Lead what they wanted.
Appoint trustworthy rebuilders.
Masculinity would be checked and have its own skyscraper.
I would live there for months.
I would return to New Society unapologetically soft and willing
I would know growth (and sweat)
I would be unafraid to call myself "man," to call myself Trans-
    gender Man
I would be a mixed Black Transgender Man
And still be soft
And willing
And not hated
And not afraid.

My art would be art and not always be "brave"
It wouldn't have to be political because of who I am.
My art would be art and not always be activism
When I wasn't even trying to be.
My art would be happy (sometimes).
People would consume my art because it was art.

I wouldn't need to put on my white woman voice to get bills paid

Or discounts

Or attention

I could just be myself

And maybe not have to pay bills

Or need discounts

but

I'll always need attention.

In a world where I feel safe, valued, and loved ... I could walk
    down the street in any neighborhood

At any time

And not wonder

If it is my

Blackness

Brownness

Racial Ambiguity

Transness

Gayness

or

Gender Ambiguity

that is killing me.

SHARYON ANITA
CHICAGO, IL, USA

I like to think I am in the process of creating such a utopia currently, but I do love visualization. In this world, I am seen for each and every one of my unique talents and gifts that I present to the world, and I am granted complete and total autonomy to utilize them when and where I deem necessary. My overall well-being is taken more into account than my amount of labor, and time to rest and meditate are understood to be of equal value to industry. We will have found a new way to guide and assist each other in finding our true contributions to society, as opposed to shaping people into class systems. Intuition, innovation, and imagination will be highly regarded in every trade.

KILAM TEL AVIV
WOODINVILLE, WA, USA

I have never given voice to this but I have always felt conspicuously unsupported by and unsafe in the world around me. For years, I have normalized and become numb to the nation's animosity toward black men. American society imposes limits on me, limitations set only by the color of my skin. To break through society's glass ceiling for black men, I must be exceptional. My gut reaction to feeling unsafe is to rebel. I rebel against any limitation or expectation set for me and push boundaries on my own terms. A world where I felt safe, valued, and loved would be one where society was equitable and supportive for all people, including me.

KENYATTA JP GARCÍA
ALBANY, NY, USA

If I felt safe, valued, and/or loved I wouldn't be the person you know of as me. I was raised up with fear. The hood was a scary place to grow up. I was brought up as disposable. Little queer negroes like me aren't worth much in this country. And I don't think I know what love is. Maybe not even platonic or brotherly love. Safe, for me, usually means being alone. My value in this world isn't about me —it's about my work. I am what I can produce. Love is a lie. I think if I could find a more ideal world for myself, I wouldn't even want to live there. I am my struggles and solitude. I don't trust safety. I devalue value and love is an extreme version of joy. I'm not here to be happy, but if others can be, I'm here for that.

ADRIENNE LA FAYE
SEATTLE, WA, USA

It was frightening for me to think that there could possibly be a world that valued, loved and kept me safe. Since I don't have an accurate reference for this type of existence, I'm petrified I would leave out things that would be my innate birthright, sadly, because I lack vision to see them. I know when I create, I could not achieve any painting success if I had no vision.

"Where there is no vision, the people will perish." [Proverbs 29:18]

Even when I attempted to imagine my made-up world, the magic was fleeting, and that in itself makes me want to weep. I didn't realize how this question would affect me. I thought it would be fun, until I couldn't see my possibilities even in my imaginary mind. Processing this question became incredibly more difficult when I thought about how the Black mother has to adjust her children's perspective at age five, so they can safely attend kindergarten and not be harmed while away from her. I can't answer this type of question because just the idea makes me feel worse knowing I might not ever achieve a glimpse of the WHAT IF I was loved, valued, and safe ...

JEN MOORE
SEATTLE, WA, USA

Imagine the energy in the magic of me was known

Imagine each nap on my head was given credit for its place in the spiral of existence for helping us swirl together so beautifully like this

Imagine my skin was akin to the black blanket that keeps the stars warm

Imagine the twinkle in our babies' eyes was called the stardust of us

Imagine knowing I am the love I seek

Imagine if the world knew I was perfect

Imagine my bills paid on time ...

I think it might feel like my shoulders easing. My molars would no longer play pestle and mortar to my dreams, grinding them down into no thing-ness. I'd like to have enough money to pay my bills on time, or at least not feel like a failure when I don't. I think the rage might subside, at least a bit, if the world took its foot off my neck long enough for me to whisper to the Earth what I had found out and that I'm sorry for what's happened. It might look like feeling no guilt about who I love and how I love. I want to love them too, but they make it so hard sometimes.

Let me get better. Imagine a world where I am safe, valued, and loved ... Sensitivity would return to the deepest reaches of us. There would be lunch breaks to stick your face in the sun and calisthenics to get us moving and flowing together. In my world, all the babies would be loved and when the new little ones were born into the world and into my family, we would revel in the darkness of their skin and praise them for reminding us of who we are. We would love the dark in my world. We would love the naps in my world. We would love in my world. Genius people would no longer need EBT.

I will keep imagining until my story is clear, until my vision comes together.

ERWIN THOMAS
BROOKLYN, NY, USA

A world where I am safe, valued, and loved is filled with youth who ask questions that adults have no fear to answer. Elders hold court on the weekend to captive audiences. Where entire communities share stories regularly. I travel with those I love to experience love in new places. I have a network of people I care for and who care for me. We work and play together. We share wealth and resources. My grandmother doesn't worry when I leave her home after sundown. There is a relaxed nature about public transportation. People in my community ask for directions, advice and wisdom. There are images and statues and stories written and told and retold about my ancestors and their contributions to humanity. There is a weekly celebration for small victories—mine or someone else's. Conversations are had under moonlight. There is no one way to be or see anything. Few ever get lost or go without food, clothing, shelter, education, or trusted community.

SHAYLA TUMBLING
ATLANTA, GA, USA

There are many ways in which I experience living in this type of world currently. I am surrounded by people who support me, and who offer space for me to learn, grow, and heal. I have pockets in all aspects of my life where we are moving together on our individual journeys and offering support and love and guidance to one another as we move. I imagine this type of community continuing to grow exponentially so that it is not isolated to tiny pockets but actually becomes towns, cities, clusters of cities and states, then full countries. In this place, I am free to be myself in all of my imperfection and awkwardness, yet am held with love, compassion, and authenticity.

KIANA DAVIS
RENTON, WA, USA

The illusion
is that we can rebuild here
But this is the place that murdered
our seeds,
our mothers,
our fathers,
and divided us so close to the bone
we can't identify where we ever connected
This is the place
that turned us into familiar strangers.
How can we heal
in the very place that wants everything we have
but nothing of who we are?

I pray for God's assurances
and search for my love, safety, and value in the words
he saved for the people called by his name.
People cursed to be blinded of their true identity
and brought in ships to strange lands to be enslaved;
I find my place in words repackaged to hide the truth in plain
    sight.
Life would be . . .
Imagine Safety . . .
When melanin is being sold . . .
and Black women are going missing . . .
harvested organs and sliced skin.

SAMANTHA HOLLINS
CLAYMONT, DE, USA

Visualization is my sharp sword combating toxic environments. I am in a bubble of brightness that ignites a combustion of zapping pressure anytime hazardous energy invades my atmosphere. I create my personal paradise like a shield that blocks off the street as soon as my body enters zones from my outside world. My inside world is a village of heart-shaped sanity that wraps its arms around my royal dark blue skin. I am crowned with luxurious serenity and blessed with lavish peace of mind when in my safe haven. We teach love (*Namaste*). We teach kindness (àṣẹ) and pass it around like a contagious condition everyone needs to acquire. My door frame is a trap that zaps all approaching *isms*. My windowpane will blast peeping green eyes to another dimension. Juju beams of light gather ancient hands to remove the residue of haters from my stoop. Sacred space is the eclipse over my holy place.

ARICKA FOREMAN
CHICAGO, IL, USA

Scraped slow with ink
everybody questions what
is a symbol other than a con-
stellation of becoming
We debate which dogmas
can withstand years as
your fingers like primas toe
hot scars with ointment until
we stand in one shadow spilled
across your bathroom floor,
home when I am want. You
salve like this   this   this, light
blinks us back to that Harlem
escape where we fired frenetic

cigarettes into the sun, talking
about our fathers, whether
the duende of making love is
incapable of apparitions or
constant in an omen's lap or
dying of clarity. These days
veils nimble, breach Bones grow
into failure. We can solve what
ambient garble news is now,
touch for the act of touching,
a need for tenderness
so small it fits at the edge
of a fingernail, at the edge
of the fingernails' edge.
At night we sleep
in the same bed, pull
breezes from our breathing.
I snore. Know safe means sleep
close to likethis &

WILLIAM WALLACE III
PHILADELPHIA, PA, USA

A safe world, in my opinion, would be one where other humans are not an existential threat. Love and value would have to fall in line for such a world to exist.

RAINA J. LEÓN
BERKELEY, CA, USA

That world exists in the spaces of my people. In those places, I am warm and fed meals made with love. I am valued for my loyalty, honesty, wisdom, and my ability to listen with love. I know and I feel how much I love them. There is always a blanket or a laugh that splits the ribs to share. There is the delight of light even in the darkest places. It's the threshold that is a site of terror and possibility for me. Cross one way to safety and care; cross another way to the "upside down" or the "sunken." And the pathways between bliss-holders are always moving, thin and electric like synapses.

CARLOS SIRAH
CHARLESTON, MS, USA

I want to stay with you in bed *always* draped in white linen with the cherry blossoms falling through your window. See the trees bloom in rapid succession? This light is thick. Your fingers pay all the proper attention to my back and inner thigh to my mons pubis to my lips.

When I bite down on your fingers you keep riding.

Later, when it is no longer spring.

I laugh, though I cannot see your face.

LAURA LUCAS
SEATTLE, WA, USA

You don't talk about moving because I bought the house next to yours. You don't try to touch my hair, without asking, without saying hello or even speaking when I walk past you. You don't expect me to do all the work that no one else feels like doing. I'm just out in the world, being myself without fear, shimmering through a star-filled sky.

TYLER KAHLIL MAXIE
CHICAGO, IL, USA

I imagine a world where queer babies run wild into the ocean. I imagine a world where queerness is everything and everyone. I imagine a world where pink is blue and blue is pink. I imagine a world where our pain is connected and our liberation is free. I imagine a world where peace is the origin of our hearts. I imagine a world where little boys can wear glitter dresses. I imagine a world where we slay every day. I imagine a world where black babies aren't killed because of their flamboyance. I imagine a world where little black gay boys can prance in the moonlight. I imagine a world where we each don't have a gender or color to represent our essence. I imagine a world where black gay boys are leaders and achievers. I imagine a world where seeing is believing. I imagine a world where glitter can stain school hallways and truly uplift those who are queer. I imagine a world where our genitalia do not define our success. I imagine a world where we each have ample opportunity to grow, prosper, and flourish. I imagine a world with pink tutus on black boys. I imagine a world where glitter falls from the sky. I imagine a world where love truly is love.

MAISHA MANSON
SEATTLE, WA, USA

The children of the panopticon have asked for hammers
    They have taken up roots, breaking glass
The children of the panopticon have asked for mortar
    They are building homes
The children of the panopticon have asked for scissors
    They are cutting each rope still dangling from trees
The children of the panopticon have been running naked
    Free of chains, free of prying eyes, no longer prey.

We are no longer prey
    We are building homes
        We are breaking glass
            We are giving way to our voice

        We are free

SHARAN STRANGE
DECATUR, GA, USA

A place of radiance and deep peace, as in a meadow mid-morning, the flush of the day begun and all its potential still vibrating within us ... Us, together, people of myriad hues, bodies, languages, cultures, beliefs, faiths, ages, abilities—yet who trust and love because it is instinctive to do so, as in a child fully open-eyed, awestruck by its existence and its mother's smell, her face, her warmth ... We enter that field each morning to work and play, with all of the animal and plant life, too ... all of us, separately and together, creative and unafraid and joyous.

JAMES E. BAILEY
FRANKFURT AM MAIN, GERMANY

I wonder what it would be like to automatically be given the benefit of doubt; that it would be assumed that I and my opinions have merit; that my contribution is worthy of consideration, even if it is ultimately rejected: to not be dismissed out of hand, and once all other options have been exhausted, to be reconsidered, and found worthy of appropriation. I wonder what the opposite of a pariah is: a paragon, revered instead of reviled. There's a reality where my skin is not a weapon, rather a virtue; an asset instead of armor. I wonder what it's like to be the default. I wonder what tenderness is like, what it's like when the world doesn't exist to calcify my exterior, to prepare me for the blows to come, but rather cradles and protects so that the slightest scratch is unbearable. I wonder what hardness feels like when all you've known is softness.

NASHELLE ASHTON
NEWTON, IA, USA

A world in which I would feel safe, valued, and loved would be a world of my people. Many different shades and depths of melanin, where we are all truly brothers and sisters and there are no overseers and we experience true freedom to love, laugh, and grow without fear of repercussion or jealousy. A worldwide community dedicated to appreciation of the magic of melanin. Where there is no fear for our children or our loved ones. Beautifully lush and everyone with a task that strengthens the world and its communities. A world built on the concept of "us" and not of "me." This would be a world I would feel safe and valued and loved in.

TRICIA DIAMOND
SEATTLE, WA, USA

A world where I am safe, valued, and loved would be one in which my ancestors exist.

There would be no discrimination of any sort, an end to sexism, racism, homophobia, misogynoir/misogyny. A world where everyone is equal versus faking it. Where I am doing work I enjoy, surrounded by friends and family and being part of a community (socializing and not isolated) who all treat each other with love and respect, having access to health care, activities, and good clean organic food and an environment where the air is clean and where I can realize my full potential and would be physically safe (because no more discrimination).

Mental health is included in health care and people are respected and thoughtful with regards to mental health care, with multicultural providers. A balance between work and home

life where relationships are seen as important (including relation-
ships with children). Where people with differences are not seen as
threats and there is an acceptance (versus a tolerance) that people
are unique and loved and the same inside as others. Also animals
are not being treated cruelly—all life is seen as important. Money
would not be the sole indicator of what provides access and acts of
generosity would show that I am valued, safe, and loved.

TIGERLILYSTAR
KANSAS CITY, MO, USA

I woke up this morning and everything was different. I opened my eyes, and for the first time, my breathing was steady. I didn't squint my eyes and wait for the reality of my lonely surroundings or the dark reminders of past hurt to press down upon me. There was no clenching of my pillows to my face to stifle the screams I often felt rising out of me every single time the last of my six alarms went off. There was none of that. Ok ... I did squint. Just a little. Old habits die hard. But this time, I slid to my back and let my fingertips creep across the bedding to the right of me. They only stopped their journey when they touched skin. Skin that wasn't mine but belonged to me. I let them linger for only a moment. Just long enough to make sure I was awake and this was my existence. I was no longer alone. For clarification's sake, the presence of a warm body in this bed isn't the only thing that changed my morning rituals from doom to, well, the complete opposite of it. But all I ever wanted was to actually have all the things that made me, well, me (my angst, my talent, my laughter, the strange way I look at the world and choose to love ...) to be received, appreciated, and needed. I just wanted to be loved and needed. Cherished. Like a child.

ANGELA BROWN
SEATTLE, WA, USA

There is a middle atmosphere that holds the fluff
There, you are free to come and go.

TAMARA BOYNTON HOWARD
SEATTLE, WA, USA

As I walk, I smile and people smile back. There is always a seat at my favorite coffee shop and no pee on the floor when I go to the bathroom. Airline tickets are free for me, so I can travel anywhere I want, whenever I want and there is always a friend nearby. My ego is assuaged and my heart is full of love. I have unwarranted confidence to live the life of freedom I deserve. Micromanagement does not exist. Not only do others trust me, but I trust myself to lean into my desires.

INTERLUDE: RITUALS

"I was 'born' into the basic goodness of Life …
into the Yes that is every portal, every door of return
and arrival, remembrance and awareness."
—Sharan Strange (Decatur, GA)

The 12 rituals included in this book were written by
Natasha Marin, curator of the Black Imagination project.

RITUAL FOR BLACK JOY

Over the phone, your sister tells you
to place one hand over your heart and smile.

She suggests you clean the house this way, left-handed with a back-
drop of Tibetan singing bowls.

She says that your babies are her babies too —
calls your daughter her nephew, your son her niece.

At the end of the day, pull your shoes off your feet
and sit on the bathroom counter to wash them in the sink.

Imagine Michelle Obama doing the same thing.

RITUAL FOR BEING UNBOTHERED

Send the email you need to send, already. Call yourself "dude" until you do it.

Stop calling yourself dude.

If you need Kuan Yin's personal blessing to be about it ...
begin with half a dozen dumplings.

Begin the next day if you must.

But the day you begin, you will know because: You will wash your feet three times in the shower with a coarse brush.

You will no longer be afraid of the night.

Violins will be like medicine if you allow them in.

Cry publicly about your generational trauma.

Use the word *nigger* on purpose because it makes everyone —Uncomfortable.

Repeat it several times.

Give in to caffeine.

Give in to nicotine.

See how gentle failure can be when people are watching.

Touch it like gravel, or a rough tooth.

RITUAL FOR BLESSING
YOUR OWN HEART

Whitney Houston's "Greatest Love of All" is the correct song to play whenever you find yourself at the end of any relationship, sexual or otherwise.

One doesn't begin with the kind of singing you have to unhinge your throat chakra for.

Work your way up to the fashions, the glitter. Practice kneeling on your ego.

Take four hours to encounter two canvases you inherited from someone else's mother.

Meet the canvas with reverence for what began in 1985—colors, lines you sweep away.

Forgo brushes for fingertips when YouTube makes a hard left, returning you to the '90s.

Cackle loudly to yourself as paint flecks your thighs.

Imagine your enemies trying to hold this tremendous joy.

RITUAL FOR REHEALING

Dress up for no reason.

Trace your eyes with liner.

Talk to your therapist about your fear of thriving.

Roll a perfect sphere of Play-Doh out during your session.
Roll away your own fingerprints with your palms flat.
Roll sticky into a dull concentric shine.

Afterwards, drive through the rain.

Listen to public radio mouth the words: *Total Destruction*.

Make it home, alive.

HEALING

"I don't need to heal myself because I'm not wounded."
—Nell Painter (Oakland, CA)

TAMARA BOYNTON HOWARD
SEATTLE, WA, USA

Therapy. 10/10 Highly recommend. I pay a woman to listen to me vent about the evils of the world. It's a bi-monthly orgasmic release of patriarchy, racism, sexism, and othering into the ether as I reclaim my oneness. As I free myself of other people's problems—I eat cake. I protect my source. I travel. I talk with my love. I pamper myself with manicures, pedicures, acupuncture, and spa dates. I forgive myself and move on.

REAGAN JACKSON
SEATTLE, WA, USA

First, I listen. This is hard when my feelings are screaming, when my body, my heart, the pieces of me are aching. Sometimes it's easier to talk, to pray, to complain, to beg, to demand. I do these things too. But then I listen and I follow. There is a guiding star that talks to me. I don't know her name or even her language. Mostly she is a dream walker of pictures, sounds, and feelings, and I awake knowing what is mine to do.

Is she ancestor or unborn child, guardian angel, spirit guide, or inter-dimensional healing practitioner—I don't know. I just know that when I listen and I follow directions, healing happens. Sometimes there is a ceremony involved. Candles or water, writing letters or burning pictures. The release of song or tears.

At these times I feel most acutely the loss of my cultural traditions. We the children of the unchosen diaspora—the progeny of the

stolen, the kidnapped, the shackled, the tortured, the enslaved—
are in many ways still lost. Lost to our heart language, lost to our
indigenous practices. We pray to white Jesus, god of colonizers,
and wonder why our prayers aren't answered. With no disrespect
to Jesus, to Buddha, to Allah, to any of the gods who come 'round
here, but we are the daughters not of Jacob and Abraham, but of
Oshun. So long estranged, I can only listen and guess, make do with
plastic cowry shells and white fabric, pray in English and hope that
there is something beyond my colonized words, that some part of
me is still me enough to be heard and healed anyway.

DARNITA L. BOYNTON HOWARD
SEATTLE, WA, USA

I heal myself through my tears, through my sacred prayers with the Divine, through laughter with loves, through whispers from waves, through stories of trees, through moonlight kisses, through child's play, and through the countless ways I've come to recognize my brilliance.

EBO BARTON

SEATTLE, WA, USA

I heal myself with words. I also hurt myself with words.

It's in the combination of words that I find hurt and healing.

There are days I allow broken glass hands to cut me.

There are days I allow clumsy, selfish, unfocused elitists in this bed.

I heal myself with poems

Words from the mouths of violins

Of fingertips

Of untouched nape.

From the words of composers

That somehow know me

That have lived lives I have yet to know

But will

That live among the stars I still worship

I invite poems to join me in my room

Provide me something more than this
Life
Enough time to pass for my skin to find my wounds
Open
And cover
Them back up.

SHARYON ANITA
CHICAGO, IL, USA

I learned early that I was at home in music. I easily get lost in various rhythms and enjoy going on the emotional journeys that each piece can take me. Having the consistent drums gives me a sense of safety and lull me into enough of a trance to either escape my current reality, or puts words to what I'm feeling when I can't do it alone.

In my last gig, I toured for eight and a half years teaching rape prevention on college campuses and military bases. By the time I left, I was only averaging three to seven days home a month. The combination of the taxing subject matter and the constant travel took a toll on my mental health. Thankfully, I discovered something called RADICAL self-care (which I don't find to be radical at all, hehe). To me, it is just the idea of doing something you LOVE for yourself—EVERY SINGLE DAY. Whether it's a favorite food, a pedi, a living room dance party, or sleeping in to a seemingly ridiculous hour, I purposely seek out something that brings me joy on a REGULAR BASIS. It's gotten to the point now that I refuse to do anything that doesn't bring me at least a modicum of joy (outsourcing does wonders with accomplishing tasks, I've found).

My favorite discovery once I started the practice of radical self-care is the more I treat myself with love, the more everyone who enters my space follows suit.

KAHN DAVISON
WESTLAND, MI, USA

For me, "healing" has been about retreating. I grew up an only child raised by conservative grandparents. I had very few friends in the neighborhood that I was allowed to play with and I always went to Catholic school instead of the neighborhood schools. I was never lonely because I had toys, imaginary friends, hip-hop music, and a vivid imagination. I started writing poems in seventh grade and I would trade them to other kids for food (and they would give the poems to their girlfriends). By eighth grade, I was checking out *Sports Illustrated* magazines from the library and drawing all the athletes. Sometimes I would take the drawing, put it in the typewriter, and write a poem over it. By ninth grade, my love for hip-hop had taken over. I was making my own mixtapes using the pause button on my boom box and then I decided I wanted to rap. So I got a microphone and a mixer for my birthday from Radio Shack.

I would write rhymes during school and then record myself when I got home over instruments (back then you could buy a single and the instrumental would be on the same side). I must have recorded over 40 hours of songs. I was in my own world and I loved it.

I'm still that kid. I still find healing and solace in the comfort of my own projects. That's why I'm such a fan of "the process of creating." That's where I go to mentally restore myself. I write, I take photographs, I make composites, and I'm in the process of learning how to make one-minute movies. The mental space I'm in when I'm creating is one of solace and utopia. No matter how much the world breaks me up—it's my creative space that puts me back together again.

KILAM TEL AVIV
WOODINVILLE, WA, USA

Writing heals me. I once read the phrase "live life intentionally." Unable to get it out of my head, I began to question what my intentions are for the world I live in. The conclusion I came to was to encourage people to share their stories. So often in life we only get the abridged version of a story filled with the agenda and personal bias of a third party's interpretation or results. It's almost impossible for anyone to accept information unless it already confirms or resonates with an experience they have already had. The "neat version" of life only serves to confirm closely-held biases and to cover over what is uncomfortable, ugly, and real. Writing allows me to share the uncomfortable realities of my experience as an African American male. I hope that through sharing my writing and reading the truth of others we can all understand the complex, painful, and beautiful world we share.

KENYATTA JP GARCÍA
ALBANY, NY, USA

I don't put much effort into healing myself. I worry that I am beyond healing. I do my best to avoid wounds but that doesn't always work. So, when I do need to heal, it's a slow process sure to leave plenty of scars. I hide behind socializing. I talk. I text. I post. I get it all out there. I lay myself bare and let the scavengers feast upon that which is good for the feasting. Then I take what is left of me and move on. I regenerate moreso than heal. I'll become whole again by being partially new. I don't forget what I've lost but I look to the future, however absurd that might be with all its repetition, and prepare myself to carry on. For me, it's all about time and exposure. I don't take space. I insert myself into social situations and hope that my problems will feel less significant. I don't trust advice but I like conversation. Words have abilities that go beyond both their meaning and intent. I put my will to exist into the care and consideration of language. Silence might be safe but it'll never save me.

ADRIENNE LA FAYE
SEATTLE, WA, USA

I regroup on a daily basis and I ask myself questions so I can innately see the right path. I try to look at the big picture and see how much I've accomplished. Stop working every minute of the day and let go of things that can't change. Once I know that I've done my best, I exhale and let things fall where they may.

The strategies that help me to heal are forgiving, forgetting, and choosing my battles. I do this for selfish reasons—for my peace of mind and for my health. So what if people don't like me, or judge me falsely? I know who I am and I'm serious when I say *I love me*. If you truly recognize me—who I am—you would at the very least like me too.

SHAYLA TUMBLING
ATLANTA, GA, USA

I cry. I laugh. I eat. I sing. I dance. I scream. I talk to my sisters.
I replay events over in my mind. I sleep. I do rituals. I engage in
ceremony.

KIANA DAVIS
RENTON, WA, USA

I am healing
because I can now see
that our flesh feeds darkness,
And others' need to hurt me
is their desperate
need to appease their invisible tormentors
that hide inside their pain and insecurities.
Forgiveness is easy
when you can see the truth
behind the masks and strongholds.

SAMANTHA HOLLINS
CLAYMONT, DE, USA

When my mind and body rebel against my spirit, I feel like I am no longer on this realm, as if I am outside of my body for the moment of emotional sickness. Sleep is the go-to drug of choice so I can give my mental space time off. Then comes the purge that replays in my mind over and over again until I dissect every reasonable thought and calculate every action. Once my flesh is able to flush out the trigger points, I submerge in water with smoke signals that lead me to the wisdom I need to begin the healing process. If I need to soak my face with a cleansing of tears, I am not ashamed. If I need to roar like a lion until I regurgitate excessive pain, then I have no regrets. If I need a pair of ears to be my personal journal, then I will not hold back my story. After I release all my demons to my angels, I open my eyes, ready to start forgiving myself for allowing unwanted energy to shift my path. I am then able to swallow the huge pill of forgiveness. I came to the realization that the longer I cuff myself with anger, the longer I punish myself for the offense against me. Instead of trying to change others, I modify my own actions so I don't inflict the same wounds on my healing heart. Sometimes you have to put up a peace sign and a middle finger simultaneously.

CHRISTOPHER BURRELL
TACOMA, WA, USA

To heal, I handle the stones that reflect my element of Earth, to help balance out my energy along with the world around. Mostly, I play songs of lyrical significance and cry. I'm currently healing now. It's been going on since the breakup. It's been since September, and the pain to my heart has sent me into a full empathetic mode.

The world around becomes magnified as I take on its pain with my own, and then I cry. I cry for my origin, I cry for my heartache, I cry to "evolve out of this shit." Afterwards, I feel light, empty, ready to be filled with new sigils and light to go on another day. That's all I can do. Crying leaves me open to hope ... and hope is healing. A natural release valve that all should access.

WILLIAM WALLACE III
PHILADELPHIA, PA, USA

To heal, I step away from my own life and seek out the places where Life is at work. Whenever possible I drive thousands of miles towards storms or forest or incalculable spaces. And I breathe. And I listen. And I let go. And I'm free.

KADAZIA ALLEN-PERRY
SPANAWAY, WA, USA

I heal myself in the comfort of consistency. I really value familiarity. I've had the same grocery list for as long as I can remember. These foods are so ingrained in me that I immediately notice when a brand has changed the recipe of one of my go-to foods. I watch television shows all the way to the bitter end, even when the show goes to trash halfway through the series. My family is my home base. Regardless of how much they drive me up the wall, they're who I can breathe the deepest with. Outside of my comfort zone live a lot of inconsistencies. A dad who was never fully present. Friends who never wanted to sleep over. Boyfriends who only saw my body. I feel most broken when my routine is interrupted. And in those moments, when I'm gasping for air, I pray for my family to grab onto me. I pray for a new episode of *Grey's Anatomy*. I pray for a bowl of hot canned peaches before bed. I pray for everything to feel okay after I've created a new normal.

ANGELA BROWN
SEATTLE, WA, USA

I shut out as much of the noise as I can.
And spend time in my internal space.
I make sure to have fun and laughs there.
But there is drama and suspense too and
Thus very cathartic.

CARLOS SIRAH
CHARLESTON, MS, USA

Remember to run if you need to. Remember the dawn and stew and buildings and *by our gods* keep record. Remember shape. Remember to forget your shape. Remember the hills wet with dew. Remember the hills wet with blood. Remember to leave the city.

LAURA LUCAS
SEATTLE, WA, USA

I breathe the air above the lake. I look at the water falling from the sky. I sleep while the sun rises. I write in the small hours of the night, when the streets below my window are empty.

TYLER KAHLIL MAXIE
CHICAGO, IL, USA

I look deeply within the pain that I suffered and I see beauty. In the deep cuts and wounds of my suffering, I see a beautiful queer God that is a healer of such pain. As I patch up my wounds, I realize that my wounds have wounds. In order for me to heal, I often try to heal others and sometimes I am met with disdain. Within this cycle of violence, I just keep on fighting against the world that tells me that this pain is normal. My bloodline runs deep and I have thickened skin upon my feet. I know that there are those before me who never saw the sunshine. My heart hurts for these ancestors as they dreamed of the life that I have. When I think about my ancestors, it makes me smile as they smile back at me and tell me to keep on fighting. I am a warrior and my healing is just a testament to my strength.

MAISHA MANSON
SEATTLE, WA, USA

Praise the goddex

Praise be the trans
The formations of reliance in your heart, in your waves.
The ones who hold you strong

Praise be the tired
Eyes sunken and weary,
The ones whose arms spread too far to catch the wind
May their burden be lessened
May you lift their head to drink

Praise be the damned who name our dead and cry their names
Who cry their names

Who name our dead
And our dead
And our dead
And our dead.

Praise be the blood seen dirty
That holds your traditions,
Drum beats them as lullabies
Praise be the words as sharp as knives
May they speak your name with pride

Praise be the goddex who sees you valid, whole,
Who live in the glimmer,
The shine in the still water

Praise the goddex who ever you are.

SHARAN STRANGE
DECATUR, GEORGIA, USA

I remember that I have the ability to heal ... that I can decide on wellness and seek it ... that I am already the wholeness that I seek. That is the vital memory, the resetting of the code of original consciousness. Meditation puts me in touch with that knowledge. I listen to my body and respect its laws ... as a system unto itself, and its relations within other fields of universal energies. And so, I consider the traps of my neuroses, my cravings. And the fear and ignorance and hate of those who torment and oppress in this world—I see their sickness and reject it. I raise my shield of self-respect and love ... or, when I find myself struggling toward it, I take sanctuary in love that has been gifted to me. I believe in the talismanic power of my grandmother's coat, her nightgown—bearing that surrogate skin, I move in grace ... her scarf pulled through my fingers, a vase from her table. These objects bear the memories and emotional energies of her love, love that heals.

NASHELLE ASHTON
NEWTON, IA, USA

I heal myself with tears. I cry alone in the shower. I open every hurt—my own and that of others—letting out in long sobs and wailing. I choose the shower to be alone and unaffected by what others may think. It feels so good to let the pain out.

TRICIA DIAMOND
SEATTLE, WA, USA

I heal myself through connecting with my ancestors through meditation, art (dance, music), and science. By focusing on my actions and reflecting on what happened, I assess what life lesson I learned through the pain. Every experience teaches me a lesson I was sent to learn, and I heal myself through seeing it through that lens and by reaching out to help others who are experiencing that pain as well. Through reflection and helping others navigate pain is how I heal myself.

KEITH S. WILSON
CHICAGO, IL, USA

I love to sing so sometimes they are lullabies.
It's not always love / I am thinking of
which is another thing about love

KAMEKO THOMAS
SEATTLE, WA, USA

The way I heal myself is by being truthful with both myself and others. It may sound like a simple thing, but the fact of the matter is that being truthful with yourself is probably one of the most difficult things for you to learn how to do—especially when it runs counter to what most people have been programmed to expect. Everyone loves the truth, until they hear it, that is. Then it's all insults, recriminations, ad hominem attacks, and breaking furniture.

It's no wonder, then, that so many people prefer the alternative; maybe it's not so much that people like lying, as it is they don't want to deal with the discomfort that comes from telling the truth. Most people aren't brave enough to grapple with that discomfort. Being truthful means creating discomfort for yourself, where otherwise none would exist—it's very tempting, then, to look the other way and make a different choice.

That's what makes being truthful so hard; that's also what makes it so healing. And that's how I work on healing myself, every day.

BRIAN BROOME
PITTSBURGH, PA, USA

Dear Ms. Dirty Look,

If we're all going to be stuck here side-by-side like black crows on a bough shivering against the winter wind while waiting for the gods of Public Transport to rescue us, I'm going to take the opportunity to bust a proverbial move. You see, the ass that I shake serves me on two completely distinct levels: 1) It is the only way that I can release the kind of perfectly sumptuous joy that only The Mary Jane Girls can dish out. 2) It keeps my nuts from freezing to my taint.

Perhaps my reverse twerk turnaround step ball change caught you off-guard and the hotness of it caused undue moisture within your industrial-strength underpants causing your face to contort and wrinkle like a fresh poop. I cannot say for sure. But, should I see you in future, please prepare yourself because, rain or shine, there is a good chance that I may just pimp, switch, and sway; and while

I appreciate your treating me to your best stankity-stank-ass-face,
I would be most anxious should you ever turn it upon me again.
Thank you for lending me your cauliflower ear.

Yours Now and Forever in Electric Boogaloo,
Brian

INTERLUDE:
RITUALS

RITUAL FOR UNBUSYING

Afternoon sun and gin whenever possible.
But on an overcast day, one might choose first:

Not to bathe.

Let the smell of you, your legs sliding open, be a reminder that you are an animal.

All the tympani of self-importance, drumming like a corrugated crown of incessant rain.

Silence is what you need now. Naps.
The sound of someone else's voice, as you read.

Unbraid and run your fingers through your own tangles. Savor every moment of this languor.

Put lemongrass on your scalp.

Orange on the soles of your feet.

RITUAL FOR BROKEN FEELINGS

If you can catch the sky when it is both pink and lavender,
you are already letting go.

You, like those tinted clouds at the horizon,
have stretched to a ribbon.

In order to zero the soul-body parallax, one must be willing
to listen to children under ten speak incessantly.

It is the only cure.
Listen to them open portals with ease.

RITUAL FOR #CAUCASIANLIVING

Pretend it is morning, late at night.
Make coffee with cream and sugar.

Consider ordering expensive flavored syrups so your home can
feel more like a cafe.

Disregard any thought of pampering as self-indulgent.

Proceed to pamper yourself, as though you are a rich white woman.
Spend too much money on organic black cherry juice.

Orange candles are difficult to find—take an afternoon
to wander aimlessly through aisles, smelling candles

like growing things.

RITUAL FOR UNERASING

Over the phone, your mother tells you about a recurring dream. You and your best friend emerge from a green building—"a house of ill-repute," mother suggests ...

"Whorehouse?" you bubble out. Mother makes a sound. She is agreeing (yes) and disagreeing with your word choice at the same time. Some psychic doorbell is ringing inside your mother. She needs you to answer it, but your thoughts are slippered and slow as they shuffle across your mind towards the door.

"I was more afraid for you than I was afraid of my own father, because when you came out of that house, you were naked—you were only five or six years old—and all over the sky, your hurt glowed low and orange. I felt it."

*   *   *

Find expensive ways to escape. Go to a bookstore. Reading is like taking notes with a pen and paper. Write a letter. Be analog while

157

you find the lead of yourself again.

Say no in a breezy way whenever you can.
Let your hair fade to lavender. Clip your toenails. Make dinner.
Coping is ever so awkward.

ORIGINS

"Whether we like it or not, we are always lovingly connected ... "
—Shay Young (Las Vegas, NV)

BRIAN BROOME
PITTSBURGH, PA, USA

Last night, I learned that I come from people who used to wash a baby in a metal tub, then dump the baby out and fill the tub with grease to fry chicken. I learned that any and every ailment, from a headache to a high fever, was cured with some plant they called "rabbit tobacco." I am less than a generation away from people whose cure for chicken pox was to lock the afflicted up in a chicken coop and make sure that each chicken in the coop jumped over the patient's head at least one time. I come from real, voodoo, country, southern black people who made me laugh last night until tears rolled down my face. I come from beautiful, witty, and intelligent people who were sold into slavery.

They talked about how they weren't able to go to doctors because all the doctors were white. They weren't able to go to doctors because they couldn't afford it. They reminisced about mothers and grandmothers who would mix sugar with kerosene and feed it to them to cure the common cold and rub chewed up plants on bee stings and cuts.

"It's a wonder they didn't kill us."

I listened to a hundred stories last night. The old folks in my family brought segregation, poverty, and racism to life and somehow made it hilariously funny. The stink of the acifidity bags steeping in hot water or hung around the neck to ward off evil spirits. They talked about long-dead aunties, and grandmamas who didn't take shit from anybody and stood on the front porches of their shotgun shacks with actual shotguns.

It was a real gift to sit and listen to them laugh and talk. I got gifts this morning, but last night's were better. I love stories. Because embedded in each story was the power of hope and belief. They believed that the chicken jumping over your head in the coop would cure chicken pox and it did. Kerosene and sugar and whatever the hell rabbit tobacco is, all did the trick.

KAMEKO THOMAS
SEATTLE, WA, USA

There are people on this planet who actively encourage the creation and distribution of chaos, because they use it—no, they need it—as the fuel to feed their dark energy. These people praise science, but vilify art. They preach the importance of kindness and generosity, yet seldom, if ever, put what they preach into practice. These people also preach that nonconformity is a sin—punishable by ostracism and a lifetime of being perpetually misunderstood. I can see how being constantly misunderstood, judged, blamed, or shamed for being wholly, uniquely one's self would make a person choose to just "go along to get along." The well-worn path is well-worn because it's easier to navigate. I, on the other hand, actually prefer the road less traveled. Because I know better.

ROBERT LASHLEY
BELLINGHAM, WA, USA

Everything about my origin story begins with my grandmother's basement. It was the bottom of the house that she bought after 25 years of working in the military laundry room and running a pool hall at night. It was the second hangout spot for her and her old friends after she was run out of the pool hall because she wouldn't give militants hush money. It was also the safest place I have ever known in my life. My grandmother found out that my father had beaten me and interceded in my life and health. She offered my mother a place where she, my grandfather, and my great aunts and uncles would babysit when my mom and aunts would work in sales shifts in order for her to get her life together. My job in that basement was to play records, make sandwiches, and listen. She taught me the meaning of music and the meaning of my history. I learned that an intrinsic part of being a black DJ and a black artist was to carry on the tradition of The Comforter. I also learned that there was no dichotomy between sophisticated art and giving black people joy. I also learned how infinitely complex Black Joy was.

My grandmother would tell me stories about the convict camps in Birmingham, Alabama in the early to mid-1930s. She told me what they would make her wear, what she worked on, and how random men would come to harass her. And if she responded, it would only mean more time for her. My grandmother was especially abused because she had run afoul of one of Birmingham's most beloved negroes—the first Bob Lashley, my grandfather in nothing but blood. He made cakes. He sang well. He espoused religion and acted docile. Bob Lashley had status in the white community. My grandmother wanting to bring charges against him was seen as a bother, while my grandfather's drinking and outbursts towards white men were sufficient cause in those white men's minds to put her in work camps on several occasions.

Bob Lashley was 25 when he encountered my grandmother. My grandmother was 12. I remember early Sunday afternoons listening to her when my dad would leave my brother and I at her house to either do business or roam the streets. And she would sit in the basement, draw the windows, turn on a little light beige lamp, and have me play her records. She would sit with my uncle Mo, smoke a pack of Kools, and have me pour her two shots of gin. She'd stare out into the brown-black of the room. She would not say a word. She would just look in the light and dark of a space that had so much history to her. And so my uncle Mo—I remember his gentle voice, his stutter. His attempt to cohere eloquence through tremendous pain in the way he listened to people, in the way, when his head was right, and he didn't need to lie down, he could read people poetry and make them feel comfortable.

He came back from World War II unable to do much except drink, write, and cook for his friends at the Caballeros Club from time to time. He was loved. Deeply loved. I remember many people coming down to the basement to take my uncle out, or have him cook for them, while I sat in the living room and listened while they talked. Suffering from PTSD, he would have days where he would be disheveled and either my grandmother, grandfather, or uncles would clean his beard and take him downstairs. On the days he would clean his own beard, his mind would be this large, interactive, improvised world of poems, ideas, and sayings. It was a place that invited other people in—and in those days, when a closed door could work, those same people were patient until it would open again. I was my grandmother's little man. I was my uncle's little buddy. I had terrible, terrible things happen in my life. Primarily, the dark and murky circumstances of how my mother would die in 1994, and the events that led to that. But, in that basement, I can't put into words how happy I was. Or how truly loved. This is my origin story.

QUENTON BAKER
SEATTLE, WA, USA

My origin story is being object and subject. Being put upon, pushed down, and pressed into something that I didn't know I needed to be or could be in order to survive to the next day or the next week. It's one of contortion—the way that I had to turn myself into different forms of refracted light just to escape the different types of gazes, grabs, hands, limbs reaching out—it's just like everything I encountered wanted a piece or part of me, wanted to take something. It felt like the origin of me was the origin of theft and I had to learn how to not be stolen from while also stealing enough to keep myself alive.

SHAY YOUNG
LAS VEGAS, NV, USA

My inheritance is light—gold and turquoise light from a time that is timeless—a space that has no space. And to come through a womb and be birthed here on Earth—that is my inheritance—the fact that I'm even here, and you're here, and we're all here. This is my inheritance. Because this didn't have to happen, you know? Each day is like that. I'm always finding myself in really groovy situations, saying damn, I didn't have to be here. I could've been sitting around depressed in my house or whatever. But the breath—me breathing is my inheritance. I think that's what keeps us going—it's the small things, the simple things that keep us going. And knowing things like there is joy in your heart—that's inheritance. And water, that's huge.

AVERY YOUNG
CHICAGO, IL, USA

The story of my origin ... Chicago, IL ... June 26th, 1974. From my understanding, Little Lily went into labor and they were rushing her to the Cook County Hospital, which was maybe a half an hour trip from where we were staying, or where she was staying ... I think she was staying with my cousin, Kitty, but I'm gonna have to ask ... Legend says that I was born in the back seat of a black Cadillac. I was already out by the time they made it to the hospital. I was already out. And the rest is BE BLACK history.

ARTEMIS OSUNA
SEATTLE, WA, USA

I didn't know what was happening—all I saw was that my eyes were like a bunch of options. It showed a description of what each child's personality would be like and what the future would be like, but it didn't tell us anything else, so I decided to do a person who was kind, mindful, and very secretive, and can sometimes be mellow, but when angry is furious, likes video games and a bunch of other technology. I was like, oh ok, I guess that sounds fun. So somehow I transported into what I wanted and all of a sudden it resumed my life as a three-year-old kid. I was just born with all of these memories just randomly in my head. And I didn't know what was going on, I couldn't speak well ... I was confuzzled. All I knew were my ABCs; how to count to five; that Easter, Halloween, and Christmas were a thing. And I knew about cake on my fourth birthday. I knew what candy was but I didn't know what a computer was. I had a ball and a few stuffed animals, but I didn't know what was going on until I realized what friends were. When I met another kid, I was like WHOA, you look just like me! We were both small and had very chubby faces and walked around like we were penguins. A few years later, I started to realize that I was starting to get a personality. I started to feel like a person. My first picture was a bunch of scribbles and a bunch of dots. I was pretty proud of myself.

EBO BARTON
SEATTLE, WA, USA

Before the tragedy of my mother meeting my father, I was salt.

I was a grain of salt in a pile on the Manila Bay dock.

Once, I was a bead of sweat on the jawline of Lapu-Lapu.

I was born from his cheekbone, traveled down to his chin as he beheaded Magellan, the ultimate resistance to Spanish colonization. I am a grain of sand Magellan's head fell to. I returned to the ocean.

Before the tragedy of my mother meeting my father, I was the ocean.

My mother traveled across the Pacific Ocean to meet her destiny in a country of false promises. I am a tear born from her eyes, when she laughed with her siblings despite their misfortunes of being immigrants in Los Angeles, California. I was the tear unborn from her eyes when they berated her English, the tear birthed from her eyes when my grandmother told her she couldn't date Black men, the sweat dripping from her forehead every time she tried to leave my father.

Before the tragedy of my father meeting my mother, I was spit.

I was the spit in his mouth when, at nine years old, he recognized that the diner did not allow Black children to sit at tables. The spit he spat, confused, when he was asked to leave after spending money there. I was the spit he spat when he played baseball, when they wouldn't let him apply for college, the spit he spat at every woman he came in contact with, the sweat from his brow when he worked in kitchens, in physical labor positions, and the spit he spat when they told him he wasn't worth spit.

My mother, a server at Bob's Big Boy; my father, the manager. She refilled the shakers with salt when their eyes met.

Just before the tragedy began, I was salt.

LAURA LUCAS
SEATTLE, WA, USA

Whenever I am not with you, I am in a library. I come from a castle of words, surround myself with bindings that peel and whisper and scent the air. I can tell you anything about anything, because the first words I learned were trying to describe the beauty of where I was.

JAMES E. BAILEY
FRANKFURT AM MAIN, GERMANY

I begin as a thought, the idea of a thought, the wisp at the beginning of an idea of a thought that will become the song that you sing when you don't care who is there to see your joy. I curve and coil around the edges of your brain, oozing and easing myself into the crannies and nooks where you are who you are regardless of who is there to try to tell you otherwise. I flit and fill and fly and fight my way through every fiber of the vessel you inhabit, flinging and folding myself into the dance that you dance because the music has filled your breath and the only exit is your fingers and your feet and your legs and your arms. I was born of the love that the sun had for your momma and the water had for your daddy. I am the steam that arose when they met.

KAHN DAVISON
WESTLAND, MI, USA

I see my life and everything that happened before it as a quintessential Detroit story; it's my origin story. My grandparents moved to Detroit from the South, looking for work, and in the process they found each other. They created my mother (and my uncle). My mother was a talented musician and scholar and was in the process of getting her master's in music (she was also an elementary school teacher and church choir director). She had me in 1976 and my father killed her and himself in 1977. My father could never seem to get over his depression and career issues.

This is the part of my origin story that's most talked about, the part I get the most questions about. But I say my actual origin started the minute my grandparents found each other on Detroit soil. I was raised by my grandparents (my mother's parents). The same lessons and standards that were taught to my mother were taught to me in almost an identical and more mature fashion.

My grandfather was the sum of his experiences. The home-made cigarettes he rolled up at 12 years old, the naked white girl he avoided so he wouldn't get lynched at 13 years old, the friend who reneged on his promise to let him stay with him when he first moved to Detroit, the racist Jewish doctor who actually wasn't racist at all, getting home right before the Detroit '67 riots, his five-year layoff from the auto factory, the day he moved his family into their dream house, my mother's ups and downs, and the day he retired. All those experiences (and more) that shaped his life ultimately determined how he was going to raise me as well.

My grandmother was different. She was made up of Bible verses and prayers but found no place for the nostalgia of her younger experiences. I believe her only goal in life was to be a blessing to everyone she encountered. She tried to hide the pride and frustration of my mother's life (and death), and she felt as if she could "pray" anything into happening.

That is my origin story. The experiences of my grandparents and every lesson they learned about life dictated how I was raised and became the compass and reference tools that I rely on the most.

KENYATTA JP GARCÍA
ALBANY, NY, USA

Before anybody knew anything about me, long before anybody got a good look at this, I was nobody, just like you were once also. I was without form. I mean, that's obvious. Of course, I had no shape yet nor function, but things change and people do too. Even before they are people. I was an idea without a holding cell but a good thought can't be set free for too long and so skin was given to a notion. I am a concept with curly hair, freckles, and bad eyesight, and nothing more. My upgrades have been denied. My body could be better but that might be too much. No one thinking wants to have to compete too hard with a perfect complexion. And most certainly cognitive cognition such as this self is better off not being able to see as well as those who see this. I am one of many or maybe few Androids. I am a biopunk experiment—an intelligently designed system. I was thought become human enough to pass, but never to succeed nor excel past my Makers, whoever they were. And I was put here merely to help. To serve. To entertain. It's been a waste of my processes and processing, but it's what I do. Was born to do.

ADRIENNE LA FAYE
SEATTLE, WA, USA

I lived on twelfth heaven with all of the other artist souls. It was a colorful magical place filled with happiness and wisdom. I didn't want to leave twelfth because I'd seen how artists struggle on earth. Every artist there knows most of their time is spent looking for that elusive funding for that, "I have to create this or I'll die" kind of project. And of course there was always another project after that one and still not enough money. So that was off-putting to me. Anyway, I was having a wonderful time: painting, playing the Hammond B3 organ, and being my beautiful spiritual self. Besides, I was exactly where I was supposed to be. Wasn't I?

Wouldn't you know it, the VERY first time I embraced the thought that it would be good if I never left twelfth—in that next minute, Saint Naomi called me to her glorious art studio loft to tell me I would be the next artist soul to leave. My specific charge was to be an African American, Artist, Author, Ex-Drug Addict, and Married Lesbian. I asked Saint Naomi, "Why was I chosen to be someone who clearly has all of the odds stacked against her?" She answered, "Because you're absolutely the only soul in the cosmos who could authentically do her justice, and not forget who and what God had created her to be."

St. Naomi also told me I would encounter obstacles one after another, but I had to look for the best in every situation. She said there must be love, wisdom, and inspiration in every piece that I create. She asked me one final question, "What is the reason for your existence?" I shouted, "MY NUMBER ONE JOB IS TO NEVER, EVA-EVA, GIVE UP ON BEING AN ARTIST." She proudly smiled because finally her hard work had paid off. St. Naomi knew my time had come, and I was ready to start living.

TAMARA BOYNTON HOWARD
SEATTLE, WA, USA

I journeyed through Fall and Winter so that I could blossom in Spring. The stars aligned just so. I traveled through lifetimes as a priest in Ethiopia, a nun in England and a Voudoo priestess in Haiti. I was born at night to my mama, my grandma and the matriarchy that molded my soul into me.

REAGAN JACKSON
SEATTLE, WA, USA

A northern woman and a southern man met twice somewhere in Ohio, once in a classroom where she was teaching, once at a party later that evening. On this they agree. Mom was talented tenth, a good girl and smart, a visionary pragmatist and third generation feminist. Dad came from the Deep South and poverty and the anger that never having a seat at the table breeds, a revolutionary fire and a fearlessness that comes from having lost too much already.

Never marry an Ω dog, they say. Date an Ω but marry an Alpha. They were married anyway in the Episcopal Cathedral in Des Moines, Iowa, where I would be baptized and spend many Christmas Eves, where I would read lessons at my grandmother's funeral and light candles for the grandfather I can barely remember.

I come from two parents who loved me, still love me, but fell out of love with one another by my second birthday, from two apartments with no pets and the same rules in different cities. Unaccompanied minors get all the honey roasted peanuts and airplane pins they want. I was a frequent flyer.

I come from anger and pragmatism, activism and scholarship. I come from northern winters and schools full of white kids, walking myself home, curling up with a good book. My imagination was my best friend. I knew I would be a writer before I even learned to read because the words made sense to me more than anything else in my life. They still do.

SAMANTHA HOLLINS
CLAYMONT, DE, USA

Sometimes I close my third eye to the iris upon my skull and beam myself home, back to where I dwelled before my earthbound experience. I see midnight dark that is a formation of my shell I now live in. I see sparks of light that I now carry with me as a reminder of who I was before I traveled through the portal, arriving in my mother's womb. My bones used to be the stones that resemble the moon. My aura used to be shimmers that mirrored images of stars. I lived light years away in a place that could only be channeled by the allure of tranquil remedies and the hypnotic vision of fire lit chemistry. I breathe in the scent of home and breathe out the reality that is my residence on the surface of this planet. I am now a doorway that has ushered others in this cycle of life with another force of existence. We come in peace until we gather enough data to take black to the motherland.

KEITH S. WILSON
CHICAGO, IL, USA

our minds have held the wet rags of our hearts
and wrung them as if to clean.

please
remind me of my name

there are absent-minded stretches
of you where i am likely to hit a deer,

the way it felt to see you
hurt, which reminded my blood to be,

a sea to drown
to mind,

you had with a stranger that amounted to nothing
but which crosses your mind from time to time,

devotionals to your face are insulting
to the body of your mind,

never mind i think it is
the kind of love that is general

but she was raising
as a family up through the ages of her mind

a muscle spasms in my foot and reminds me
of my heart

it is how a country loves
its people, and the back of its mind

CHRISTOPHER BURRELL
TACOMA, WA, USA

I was born from the concept of Tesla's key to the universe. The sequence three, six, and nine. Me being a three, the third son, born in the third season, of the third day of the ninth month, I was surely destined to be part of the fabric of life. Before birth, I was a part of a place that promised that when I entered this world all would be alright. Where I resided, I felt a warm glow that daily reminded me that the place I would enter would be full of love and light. To the contrary.

Entering this place left me somewhat broken and weakened. During the younger days, my frame was beaten while my mind was assaulted for existing. Through the words and beatings, I was rendered weak and helpless to overcome the people who were "destined" to watch over my mortal form. Only two, high priestesses and of no kin, watched over me. Even in death they still do, guiding my spirit.

To become stronger, I studied. To become better, I dreamed. To become more powerful and to recall my strength, I learned sigils and spells. Today, I stand remembering my past, before this time and during this time. Today, even though I wear protective sigils upon my body, and even though I have sway with spell work, I continue to feel, periodically, the state of being weak, helpless, and alone. Those bouts of weakness make me stronger, though I wish they would end. I can be strong with them.

JEN MOORE
SEATTLE, WA, USA

I was in my mother before black was laid upon existence before light came to keep it company before there was a place to be and a fire to traverse I was in my mother swirling together in the fragrance of her womb always big enough for me inside our outside of understanding before there was me I was in my mother she is me and I have always been with me before what was other came to be I was in the womb of a wombed man named Norma Jean spoken or felt her name has never changed stretched like marks around the waistlines of stars I was in my mother before being was being and before fore was ored for more when one was enough I was nestled tough in the womb of a rhododendron seed who blew her essence across mountain land and sea you see what I mean in an archetype's dream Norma Jean found me and placed me inside of her before her was distinct and womb was heartbeat she found me in the silence of infinite Being and became two know me Norma Jean loved me before fore was locked in the prison WARD of future before being be and came into plurality I was with her I am with her before I was in my mother's womb I was in my mother's heart see Norma Jean dreamed me and grafted me from the fibers of her being spent eons beyond Infinity composing the song of me until our symphony could be heard materially she gave me to this world not a second before it was ready for me see we that's me and Norma Jean been doing this thing eternally where was I before I was in my mother's womb where was the sun before the moon where was life before love bloomed we are simultaneously constructed in this ONE love when ex-is-tense thought we thought she and she thought me. We have never been apart.

NATASHA MARIN
SEATTLE, WA, USA

Many stories begin, "once upon a time," but this one begins, "despite and beyond time."

Can you remove time from this narrative entirely?

Can you spread the idea of one distinct origin across all potential temporal directions, well beyond past and future?

Can you visualize the concurrent bursting into existence across all possible points of time for one individual?

Despite and beyond time, I am.

In this way, I am both the creator and the created. I am also the witness. My lifetime is a portion of my existence, but there is no totality there. A caterpillar is a past-tense butterfly and a butterfly is a future-tense caterpillar. With or without wings, more than one reality can exist when temporality is not centralized.

So despite and beyond time, there is at all times a black woman who is creating herself. Knees bent, palms open, her focus is her power. Whatever she realizes comes into manifestation before her. She must also consistently witness herself in order to continue to exist. She is her own god out of necessity. Without her, there is nothing, no story to record. Here she is now, in your mind's eye— humming deep in her belly a joyful song that doesn't rely on words. Weaving. The bright patterns that emerge from her fingertips are the fruit of our entire existence. The cosmic fabric she weaves is made of thread, or binary code, or ancient DNA gene sequences, or something else entirely.

Substance is the material of everything around us. We are unlimited by the limits of our current understanding of our abilities. We persist. We have persisted. We will continue with or without acknowledgement.

CODA:
RITUALS

RITUAL FOR UNENDING

Let yourself be overcome by the spirit of decluttering.
Be wild in your need for space.

Look at something precious. Ask: *Why?*

Yank it up from the place where it has been resting, for years.
And carry it away from you to a ledge.

Call to one you love from the ledge.

Together, on the count of three—Toss your dusted precious
wedding broom into the neighbor's yard, saying thrice:

Kindling for a new flame.
Kindling for a new flame.
Kindling for a new flame.

RITUAL FOR REMOTHERING

Children can fill you with fear
like a new blade. Something untouched

That shines. The panther inside tongues the shape around it.
They don't know what to be afraid of yet.

After your voice has fallen in front of you
gutted at angles like some dead drug dealer's girlfriend—

Don't waste time feeling ashamed. Take a shower. Wash the blood
off your broken body with a white cloth and apple cider vinegar.

Alone in a room, tell yourself:
Get it together.

When they say:
Mommy, you are so nice today, listen.

Eat plain Greek yogurt with the most luxurious honey you can find.
Wake up to the sound of someone who believes you are better.

Be better.

Keep the laundry going so you can sleep when you finally fall.
Imagine you have whiskers as you drift to sleep.

Wake naturally.

RITUAL FOR RE-REMEMBERING

There once was a rabbit not among those gathered in the big house.
After hawk took his head, wolf his leg and arm, and coyote the rest—

His heart, like an instrument, still sang out.

Make yourself whole in this way—
with a sound that won't be ignored.

Sing until your stomach growls. Then eat.
If your sorrow needs to be heard, burn cedar.

Mix the ash with your spit.
Cover your eyelids with this shadow.

Speak like you are dreaming.

RITUAL FOR UNCERTAINTY

At the end of the summer coconut oil solidifies.
Find a way to wet yourself down like a plant in the sink.

When you have treated your body with a cloth and soap, pat dry.
Seal yourself with thick creams and the smell of cardamom.

Moisturize and decolonize. Moisturize and decolonize.
Moisturize and decolonize.

If you do not gestate, you cannot heal.
Let a pinch of pink salt pool under your tongue.

See how long it takes you to give in and swallow.
Ask a child: *Where do you come from?*

Kadazia Allen-Perry, a queer, disabled, Black woman, dares to want more than just her next breath. Deciding that surviving wasn't enough she set out to be a full-time freelance multimedia artist. She strives to explore the intersectionalities within Black identities that go beyond the blueprints laid out in mainstream representations of Blackness. Kadazia constructs stories based on the foundational elements of identity through digital film and tactile mediums. She intends to use the lens and other artistic tools as points of access for marginalized communities to command their own narratives and folklore. Her dream isn't to be rich or famous. Kadazia simply wants to make enough to fund her next artistic project and along the way build an empire that services those who are most often overlooked, because they tend to have the biggest imaginations.

Nashelle Ashton is a 48-year-old black woman originally from Dallas, Texas now residing in Iowa. She has 2 grown girls, 6 grands (and one on the way) and 4 cats. She has always wished to be creative and is finally ready to push through her fears and nurture that part of herself.

James E. Bailey is originally from Los Angeles, California. He graduated with a degree in music composition from Cornish College of the Arts in Seattle, Washington. He has performed in productions ranging from *Evita* and *Mame* to *The Marriage* *of Figaro* and *The Magic Flute*, and in choirs in both the US and Germany.

Quenton Baker is a poet, educator, and Cave Canem fellow. His work has appeared in *The Offing, Jubilat, Vinyl, Poetry Northwest* and elsewhere. He is the recipient of the 2018 Arts Innovator Award from Artist Trust, and the author of *This Glittering Republic* (Willow Books, 2016).

Ebo Barton is a Black and Filipino, Transgender and Non-Binary poet. Currently residing in Seattle, Washington by way of Los Angeles, California, they've stopped trying to understand the locally produced whiteness in the PNW. Ebo believes in the power of language and art as a tool for revolution. *www.ebobarton.com*

Tamara Boynton Howard is a high school teacher and the host of *I'm Not Your Mama* podcast. She regularly discusses things many parents never tell their kids about sex. Tamara is a beginner artist and loves to draw, listen to Kpop, and watch dramas.

When she's not crafting healing beauty potions for her organic skin and hair care line, or contemplating why most of her writings take place in her head, **Angela Brown** is working diligently to raise awareness around issues of equity and intersectionality in art making and arts education communities in Seattle.

Christopher Burrell was born in Detroit, and raised in Chicago. As a resident of the Pacific Northwest for 9 years, he uses various art forms for healing and expression as a communications professional, part-time DJ, (under the moniker Ninja Kat), and as a solitary practitioner of the craft.

Sharyon Anita Culberson is an actor and activist with a passion for travel and personal expression through the arts. She strives use music, humor, and storytelling to educate the masses, break generational curses, and encourage as many love-based political acts as possible.

Kiana Davis is an author, poet, performing artist, and educator. She has written two collections of poetry *Digging For Roots* and *From These Roots Up*. Kiana has a heart for empowering youth and teaches poetry workshops that explore class, identity, gender norms, poverty, and social justice. She is the recent recipient of a 4Culture Arts grant and will be publishing a poet collection of Black women, teens, and girls telling their hair stories.

Kahn Santori Davison is from Detroit, Michigan. He is formerly an art columnist for *The Gazette News* and Arts and Entertainment writer for the *Michigan Citizen*. He's currently a music writer for the *Detroit Metro Times*. He's served as a creative writing instructor at Detroit Impact Community Center and Inside Out Literary Arts and is a 2015 Kresge Literary Arts Fellow. Davison is the author of *Blaze* (Willow Books).

Tricia Diamond is a choreographer, government administrator, and educational consultant. New Orleans musician and manager Billy Diamond and Shirley Diamond's daughter, she is the creator of New Orleans Bounce fitness brand Seattle Twerkshop as well as a public administrator completing her doctoral studies in public agency leadership at Seattle University.

Aricka Foreman is a poet, essayist and educator from Detroit, MI. Author of *Dream with a Glass Chamber* (2016) and *Salt Body Shimmer* (forthcoming from YesYes Books), she has received fellowships from Cave Canem, Callaloo, and the Millay Colony for the Arts. Her poems, essays and and visual-praxis-features have appeared in *The Offing*, *Buzzfeed*, *Vinyl*, *RHINO*, *James Franco Review*, *THRUSH*, *Please Excuse This Poem: 100 New Poems for the Next Generation* (Viking Penguin) among others. She lives in Chicago.

Kenyatta (aka Kenning) JP García is the author of *OF (What Place Meant)*, *Slow Living*, and *Yawning on the Sands*. Xe is a diarist and performer. Xe studied linguistics and was a cook for many years. Now, xe works overnights cleaning floors trying to make enough money to get to the next gig. Hopefully, a paying gig cuz exposure ain't never paid no bills.

Samantha Hollins, aka rock singer/songwriter/guitarist GhettoSongBird (since 2001) from Philadelphia, started expressing her soul through writing poetry, short stories, and songs at the age of 8. She attended the Art Institute of Philadelphia in 1994–96, earning a music/video business associates degree. Scripting writing, songwriting and creative writing classes polished her vivid knack for storytelling. In 2012 she wrote a short film to accompany her "Alley of The Earth" music video. Two years later she was commissioned to write her unique style of Rock music reviews, announcements with UNHINGED MUSIC out of Maryland. In 2016 she became a guest writer with *moviemusicthoughts.com* in Philadelphia reviewing horror films. Writing songs, however, is her never-ending story.

Darnita L. Boynton Howard is an interdisciplinary artist and designer. With an obsession of patterns in tow, she creates fractals, textiles, and paintings to explore nature, cosmic design, culture, and spirituality. Her purpose is to bring more awareness about the beauty and wonderment residing in self and the world.

Adrienne La Faye is a painter, filmmaker, and community social justice arts educator focused on chronicling the African American Diaspora. Born and raised in Seattle, La Faye is a narrator-driven artistic-historian, an activist, and same-gender married woman. La Faye works to defend the disenfranchised and the marginalized against systemic racist judicial systems. She is the author and illustrator of the book, *Dream Jumpers the Inheritance*.

Raina J. León, PhD, is the author of three collections of poetry, *Canticle of Idols* (2008), *Boogeyman Dawn* (2014) and *sombra: dis(locate)* (2016) and the chapbook, *profeta without refuge* (2016). She is a co-founding editor of *The Acentos Review*, an online quarterly, international journal devoted to the promotion and publication of Latinx arts. She is an associate professor of education at Saint Mary's College of California.

Laura Lucas (she/her) is a VONA/Voices fellow and a poet, fiction writer and essayist of Polish and African-American descent. Her writing has appeared in *Bards And Sages Quarterly*, *Supernatural Tales*, *Graffiti*, and *Rigorous*, among others, and can be found at *lauralucas.net*.

Maisha Banks Manson is a Queer, gender non-conforming, Black identified artist, activist, teacher and writer. They have devoted their personal journey to self healing through reclamation of personal history, knowledge and creating spaces for healing of others.

Tyler Kahlil Maxie is a 23-year-old, nongenderconforming artivist who was born in the city of Chicago. Although his origin may stem from violence and oppression, his light and love can be seen through all of his works, whether they be theatrical, poetic, and/or spiritual. God is king.

Jennifer Moore is a poet and multi-disciplinary artist born and raised in the Northwest, with a focus in music and sound. She draws inspiration from daily life. She creates as a practice of love and freedom. She believes sharing to be an integral part of growth and healing. She believes blackness is a light left on for the world to come home to itself.

Carlos Sirah is a native of the Mississippi Delta. He is a writer, performer, and cultural worker. Sirah creates formal structures rooted in Black expressions of possibility which manifest and operate across disciplines. Sirah holds an MFA in Writing for Performance from Brown University and is a Macdowell Colony Fellow. A longer version of Sirah's text here will be published in a forthcoming book, *The Light Body & The Utterances: A Tête Bêche* (The 3rd Thing, February 2020).

While many poems come off like a lecture, or someone airing out their grievances, **Kilam Tel Aviv**'s poetry is a relationship. He grapples the harsh realities of the world with caution, ferocity and the honesty. You can find more of Kilam on Instagram for weekly poems @kilamtelaviv and *speakerthoughts.com*.

Erwin Thomas (Baba Ifasanmi Fayemi), is a child of Cecelia and Edward Thomas. Grandchild of Eunice & Andrew & Cleopatra & Samuel. Erwin is a professional international artist, educator, spiritual & creative consultant whose ongoing work includes the use of various transformational disciplines to engage various villages globally in sharing knowledge and exploring brave new ideas around cultivating wellness, creativity, historic legacy, cultural identity, restorative practices, and sustainable community.

Kameko Thomas, M.A., understands the unique relationship between storytelling and healing, better than most. Storytelling is what gave her the courage to share her experiences as a Black Woman veteran living with PTSD—an intersection of race, gender and disability hardly—if ever—discussed.

Tigerlilystar, known in music as Angel Gibson, is a creative singer, who has been in the eclectic pop band, My Brothers & Sisters, for over 8 years. When she is not busy with music, she is fully focused on her energetic daughter McKenzie, writing poetry, short stories, and dancing.

Sharan Strange's poems and essays have been published in numerous journals and anthologies in the U.S. and abroad—most recently in *Furious Flower: Seeding the Future of African American Poetry*. She has also created sonic and visual art-based works for museum and gallery exhibitions in New York, Boston, Oakland, Seattle, and Atlanta, and her collaborations with composers have been performed by the International Contemporary Ensemble, the American Modern Ensemble, and The Dream Unfinished Orchestra, among others. Her honors include the Barnard Women Poets' Prize (for her collection, *Ash*), the Rona Jaffe Foundation Writers Award, and Georgia Author of the Year Award from the Georgia Writers' Association. She teaches writing at Spelman College.

Shayla Tumbling is a mental health therapist, sexuality & emotional empowerment coach, healing facilitator, and professional platonic cuddler. She supports clients in developing healthy relationships with themselves and others. Her coaching style is integrative, holistic, sex-positive, empowerment based, compassion centered, and trauma-informed. She creates sacred spaces for clients to cultivate their emotional health & self-development. Her work centers around supporting Black Women in aligning with their personal power through healing Ancestral & Cultural Shame and Trauma and its impact on their sexuality, emotional health, and self-image.

William Wallace III is a Black artist and educator currently working in Philadelphia. Through the use of abstract portraiture and found materials, he expresses the internal schema of people

trying to maintain in this moment of socio-political upheaval.
Scrap wood from new developments, stretched bed sheets, and
early 20th-century windows from neighborhoods in the early
stages of gentrification have been some of his favorites since
moving to West Philadelphia in 2013. These materials hold his-
tory and the figures in his paintings feel like ghosts haunting our
shifting landscapes.

Keith S. Wilson is an Affrilachian Poet, Cave Canem fellow,
and recipient of an NEA fellowship. Keith serves as Assistant
Poetry Editor at *Four Way Review* and Digital Media Editor at
Obsidian Journal. His first book, *Fieldnotes on Ordinary Love*, was
published by Copper Canyon in 2019.

Serenity Wise is a Black woman in this world looking for a
place to exist.

ACKNOWLEDGEMENTS

Black Imagination would not be as sacred as it is without the brilliance of Black womxn like Nana Twumasi (editor) and Vanessa German (cover artist), who love themselves enough every day to show up with radical generosity.

ABOUT THE CURATOR

Natasha Marin is a conceptual artist whose people-centered projects have circled the globe and have been recognized and acknowledged by *Art Forum*, the *New York Times*, the *Washington Post*, the *Los Angeles Times*, and others. In 2018, Marin manifested *Black Imagination: The States of Matter*, *The (g)Listening*, and *Ritual Objects*—a triptych of audio-based conceptual art exhibitions in and around Seattle, WA. *Black Imagination* is community-based, ongoing, and continues to amplify, center, and hold sacred a diverse sample of Black voices, including LGBTQIA+ black youth, incarcerated black women, black folks with disabilities, unsheltered black folks, and black children. Marin's viral web-based project, *Reparations*, engaged a quarter of a million people worldwide in the practice of "leveraging privilege," and earned Marin, a mother of two, death threats by the dozens. This is how she healed herself.

www.black-imagination.com